make it your Style™

D1468341

ISBN: 978-0-696-24114-7

contents

"Step up to a Sizzix shape-cutting machine to discover your own creative style."

—THE ELLISON DESIGN TEAM

beth

debi

deena

cara

sizzix style

BY CARA MARIANO

It's all about *stuff*. You know, the stuff that catches your eye in the aisles of your favorite creative hobby store, catalog, or Web site.

The stuff that makes you think, "What am I going to do with all this stuff?"

It's this kind of stuff that drove us to collect our very best thoughts and present them to you in this very special book. Put simply, this book challenges you to turn that stuff into die-cut treasures that say so much about you!

From unique projects for your personal fashion and home décor to scrapbooking and cardmaking, each chapter explores a new and versatile perspective about a specific Sizzix

product, covering everything from machine capabilities and shape-cutting basics to the coolest ideas and techniques. So whether you decide to add just a small die-cut title to a card or the perfect word to create a custom sweatshirt, the final result will reflect your style right down to the very last rhinestone.

As you come to rely on this book for inspiration, I hope you enjoy these projects as much as I do. They were created by myself and the talented team of Ellison artists who continue to amaze me every day. Their passion makes anything possible. And, like life itself, when you love what you do, everything else comes easy!

cara mariano
ART DIRECTOR

Cara has been scrapbooking for more than 10 years and currently spends her days working as Art Director for Ellison. She enjoys spending time with her husband, Glenn, and taking pictures. Cara also loves going to the beach, which she is able to do quite often since she lives in warm and sunny Southern California. When she's not relaxing on the beach, her free time is spent scrapbooking. She describes her scrapbooking style as clean and simple, with the focus on the pictures. She has a passion for pink cardstock, and her favorite scrapbooking subjects are her friends and family.

cara's biggest inspiration:

"Everyday life—it might be a favorite T-shirt, a decorating magazine, or paint at the home improvement store—creativity is everywhere."

beth reames
SENIOR CRAFT DESIGNER

In her 15-plus years in the scrapbooking industry, Beth has lost count of the idea books and magazines to which she has contributed. She worked as an EK Success product designer for eight years and also partnered with a friend to create the Border Buddy template line. She has been with Ellison since 2005. Beth and her husband, Randy, have four teenagers in the house and find that the kids and their friends provide plenty of scrapbooking photo ops. Beth says the worst thing about scrapbooking is when the time comes to clean off her desk!

beth's favorite technique:

"I love to apply adhesive to fabric, then die-cut it, and adhere it to garments like jackets, sweatshirts, and jeans to make a fashion statement."

debi adams
CRAFT DESIGNER

Debi is no stranger to the scrapbooking industry; she's been scrapbooking for more than 14 years and has designed a variety of embellishments and dies. When she isn't scrapbooking, she enjoys sewing unique fashion and home décor items, as well as creating custom wall murals. Debi has four daughters: Kristen, Chellie, Lauren, and Alyssa, and she loves to spend her free time watching them dance. She and her family reside in Anaheim, California.

debi's favorite tip:

"Never be afraid to create something unique and new. The worst that can happen is that you have to start over, but you will have gained something in the process."

deena ziegler
CRAFT DESIGNER

Deena has always stored memorabilia in albums but has been "officially" scrapbooking for 11 years now. Her favorite scrapbooking subjects are her daughters, Niguel and Kylah, and she will always set aside time to scrapbook when they are willing to join her. Deena and her husband, Randy, also have collected many travel photos through the years, which she enjoys scrapbooking. Her style is to embrace a lot of color contrast, to place items on her page randomly and unintentionally, and to fill her pages with little details.

deena's go-to tool:

"I can't live without my hot-glue gun! I always have it ready to attach die-cuts and accents on the fly."

machines & accessories

THREE MACHINES. ENDLESS POSSIBILITIES. Open the door to creative freedom with a Sizzix shape-cutting machine. Three versatile machines—the all-purpose Big Shot™, the compact and portable Sidekick®, and the ever-popular original Sizzix® Machine give you the flexibility to add personal flair to any project. Together with a complete collection of stamps, rub ons, and die-cutting and embossing accessories, you'll be able to express yourself effortlessly.

sidekick

sizzix

system comparison

SIZZIX DIES, EMBOSSING FOLDERS & TEXTURE PLATES	DIE TYPE	SIZZIX®, BIG SHOT™, OR BIGKICK™ MACHINE	PROVO CRAFT® CUTTLEBUG™ MACHINE	QUICKUTZ® REVOLUTION™ MACHINE
Originals™	Steel blade	YES	YES	NO
Bigz™	Steel blade	YES	YES	NO
Sizzlits®	Chemically etched metal with strong plastic back	YES	Most designs	NO
Movers & Shapers™	Steel blade	YES	NO	NO
Bigz XL	Steel blade	YES	NO	NO
Decorative Strip™	Chemically etched metal with strong plastic back	YES	Most designs	NO
Clearlits™	Chemically etched metal with strong plastic back	YES	YES	NO
Emobsslits™	Chemically etched metal with strong plastic back	YES	YES	NO
Simple Impressions®—2" folder	Removable metal stencil with plastic counter die	YES	NO	NO
Simple Impressions—4" and 6" folders	Removable metal stencil with plastic counter die	YES	YES	NO
Texturz™	Plastic with silicone rubber	YES	NO	NO
Texture silicone rubber with other brands' metal stencils	Plastic with silicon rubber	YES	NO	NO
CUTTLEBUG DIES & EMBOSSING FOLDERS				
Cutting dies (all sizes)	Cast aluminum alloy	YES	YES	NO
Embossing folders	Plastic	YES	YES	NO
QUICKUTZ DIES & EMBOSSING FOLDERS				
Dies (all sizes)	Chemically etched metal	YES	YES	YES
GooseBumpz (embossing stencils)	Chemically etched metal	YES	YES	YES
OTHER SIZZIX DIE FEATURES	NOTES			
Ejection foam already assembled	No die assembly required	YES	YES	NO
Cuts 80-lb. adhesive-backed cardstock	With adhesive backing	YES	YES	YES
Ability to cut a wide variety of materials, such as cardstock, fabric, craft metals, and more	Originals, Bigz, and Cuttlebug dies	YES	YES	NO
Alphabets have color-coded, strong plastic back with label	For easy organization	YES	NO	NO
OTHER SIZZIX MACHINE FEATURES	NOTES			
Machine base works on textured, fabric-covered, or smooth working surfaces	Less movement and slippage	YES	NO	YES
Six-point wide base stabilization	Big, stable work surface	YES	NO	NO
Unibody cast-roller frame and solid core rollers	Controls flexing of machine	YES	NO	NO
Machine purchase includes Multipurpose Platform with illustrated instructions	Visual instruction reminder	YES	NO	NO
COMPONENT WARRANTY	NOTES			
Machine		3 YEARS	1 YEAR	1 YEAR
Dies		3 YEARS	1 YEAR	2 YEARS

machines

SIDEKICK

Just turn the handle on the compact **Sidekick Machine** to create a variety of creative shapes and embossed images using Sizzlits Dies and Simple Impressions Embossing Folders. A vacuum-seal feature attaches the machine to virtually any surface for easy portability.

For even more versatility, choose from a wide range of accessories, including a standard Cutting Pad pair, a 13" Decorative Strip Cutting Pad pair, and the handy Working Platform. There also is an available adapter that allows you to convert thin dies from other brands for use in the Sidekick.

Sidekick Die Compatibility
- Sizzlits
- Sizzlits Decorative Sets
- Sizzlits Alphabet Sets
- Decorative Strip Dies
- Clearlits
- Embosslits
- Simple Impressions

BIG SHOT

When you want big-time versatility, big designs, and big results, the **Big Shot/BIGkick** is a die-cutting machine that really delivers. The largest die-cutting machine in the Sizzix family, it works with the complete line of Sizzix products to give you the best range of shape-cutting options possible.

Add more versatility to the Big Shot Machine with a wide range of accessories, including a standard Cutting Pad pair, a 13" Decorative Strip Cutting Pad pair, an Extended Spacer Platform, a Multipurpose Platform, a Premium Crease Pad, and Simple Impressions Folders with Glue Tabs.

Big Shot Die Compatibility
- Sizzlits
- Sizzlits Decorative Sets
- Sizzlits Alphabet Sets
- Decorative Strip Dies
- Clearlits
- Embosslits
- Originals
- Bigz
- Simple Impressions
- Texturz

ORIGINAL SIZZIX MACHINE

The ever-popular and versatile press-style **original Sizzix Machine** utilizes Originals and Sizzlits dies to cut a variety of shapes, letters, and numbers. Use it with Simple Impressions dies for quick and easy embossing on a variety of paper types.

Sizzix Machine Die Compatibility
- Sizzlits (select designs)
- Sizzlits Decorative Sets (select designs)
- Sizzlits Alphabet Sets (select designs)
- Clearlits
- Embosslits (select designs)
- Originals
- Simple Impressions

dies and accessories

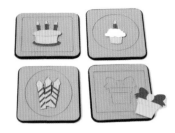

EMBOSSLITS

Embosslits do double the work by cutting and embossing in one simple step. Take your decorative shapes to the next level by adding an embossed edge to your designs.

TEXTURZ

Texturz transform the surface area of ordinary papers and other materials to create a variety of textured shapes, patterns, and words. Add instant appeal to plain paper by adding a tactile element.

SIZZLITS

These thin dies work in every Sizzix shape-cutting machine and are available in a variety of designs to suit almost any occasion. Single Sizzlits are individually packaged so you can select the perfect die for your project. Choose a four-die Sizzlits Decorative Set when you want a coordinated package of dies. Or, for the ultimate versatility, use a 35-piece Sizzlits Alphabet Set for your lettering needs.

BIGZ

When you want to be bold, nothing less will do than the big, bold style of the Bigz decorative dies. A variety of shape, alphabet, and envelope dies that can cut through almost any crafting material will help push your creative boundaries to the limit.

ORIGINALS

These dies cut swiftly and evenly to create perfect shapes every time you use them. The Originals are available in small, medium, and large sizes, so there is no limit to your creativity.

MOVERS AND SHAPERS

Get two cuts in one with these revolutionary dies. Just place the smaller die inside the larger die opening for a perfectly positioned shape within a shape.

CLEARLITS

Clearlits are designed to help you make the most of your photos. A see-through backing on the die allows you to see exactly what's being cropped from your photo so you're sure to get the perfect cut every time.

SIMPLE IMPRESSIONS

Take embossing to a new level. Just slide the stencil and material to be embossed inside the folder and run them through the machine. Use it over and over for quick embossed effects.

CLEAR STAMP MOUNTS

Use these see-through mounting blocks to easily position clear stamps for a perfectly aligned image each and every time. An aligning guide makes things even easier with a grid visible from both sides of the mount.

RUB ONS

These rub ons quickly and easily transfer to virtually any surface to complement a number of Sizzlits designs or look great when used on their own. Choose from a variety of alphabets, backgrounds, and other shapes.

CLEAR STAMPS

These see-through shapes make stamping a breeze. Simply place them on a clear mounting block for perfect placement on your craft projects whenever you stamp.

LITTLE SIZZLES

These cardstock packs are made to conveniently fit the dimensions of the Sizzix machines for ease of use and so you don't have to worry about wasting paper. Each style of paper is available with an optional adhesive backing, and the papers are offered in a wide variety of finishes and color schemes.

HOW DO I USE THE MACHINES TO CUT?

CUTTING IS AS EASY AS ONE, TWO, THREE. All you have to do is decide which style suits your paper-crafting needs. Roller-types, including the Sizzix Sidekick, Big Shot, and BIGKick machines, feature a crank handle and require a few easy turns to feed the materials underneath the roller.

Or opt for the original Sizzix Machine, which features a press-style handle that applies even pressure onto the die to cut through a wide variety of materials. Depending on your cutting needs, you'll need to make sure that you have the correct companion accessories, such as multipurpose platforms, decorative strip cutting pads, and embossing folders to ensure your success.

originals
& bigz

CHAPTER TWO

When it comes to die-cutting, versatility is a big deal. Sizzix Originals and Bigz dies are compatible with the Sizzix Big Shot, BIGkick, and original Sizzix machines, so you can create amazing shapes to take your projects to a whole new level.

supplies

- ☐ Sweater
- ☐ Felt
- ☐ Paper-backed fusible web: HeatnBond
- ☐ Iron
- ☐ Embroidery needle
- ☐ Embroidery floss
- ☐ Buttons

2

STEP TWO: Using contrasting embroidery floss and an embroidery needle, blanket-stitch around the edges of the felt pieces.

3

STEP THREE: Remove the paper backing from the felt shapes. Fuse the felt pieces to the sweater using a warm iron. Layer smaller Flower shapes on top of larger shapes and fuse in place. Hand-sew buttons to the centers of the Flowers. Add chain-stitch details for Flower stems.

Flower Layers #3

Leaves #3

appliqué sweater

Appliqué has never been this easy!
Instead of cutting out each felt piece for this sweet sweater by hand, fusible web and flower- and leaf-shaped dies make the appliqué process both speedy and fun.

essentials

- ☐ Sizzix® Big Shot™ (#655268)
- ☐ Sizzix Originals™ Dies: #654979 Flower Layers, #654982 Flower Layers #3, #655225 Leaves #3

instructions

1

STEP ONE: Using a warm iron, apply paper-backed fusible web to the back of the felt. Die-cut the Flowers and Leaves from the felt.

visual guide

Flower Layers

butterfly baby mobile

Mesmerize your little one as they drift off to sleep with this
fanciful butterfly mobile. Hearts and Fleur de Lis transform into wings and
butterfly bodies to create these irresistible winged creations.

essentials

- ☐ Sizzix® Big Shot™ Machine (#655268)
- ☐ Sizzix Originals™ Dies: #655167 Fleur de Lis; #654980 Flower Layers #2; #654982 Flower Layers #3; #654983 Hearts, Tipsy
- ☐ Sizzix Sizzlits® Dies: #654749 Build a Flower Set

supplies

- ☐ Cardstock: Bazzill Basics Paper
- ☐ Xyron machine and adhesive
- ☐ Wire: Artistic Wire
- ☐ Glitter: Sparkle n Sprinkle
- ☐ Hole punch: Fiskars
- ☐ Buttons
- ☐ Ribbon: Offray
- ☐ Beads
- ☐ Magnet: Available at Sizzix.com
- ☐ Scallop-edge scissors

instructions

To make butterfly bodies, snip off side and bottom details from two die-cut Fleur de Lis. Sandwich two large die-cut Hearts between the body layers on each side for wings. Adhere glittered curlicues and punched circles on wings; finish with curled-wire antennae.

Construct hanger from cardstock strips and cut scalloped edges on the strips. Embellish with Flowers made from layering Flower-shaped dies and buttons. Tie mobile with ribbon. Hang butterflies and a layered Flower with ribbon and beads; attach magnets to the undersides to balance the mobile. Hang mobile out of reach of children.

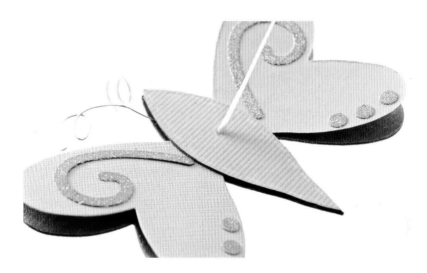

visual guide

Fleur de Lis

Flower Layers #2

Flower Layers #3

Hearts, Tipsy

Build a Flower Set

embellished flip-flops

Take ordinary sandals a step above the rest

by adding beaded accents to durable, die-cut leather shapes and

adhering them to the center of the straps.

essentials

☐ Sizzix® Big Shot™ Machine (#655268)
☐ Sizzix Bigz™ Die: #655139 Decorative Accents #6

supplies

☐ Leather
☐ Decorative metal
☐ Extra-strong adhesive
☐ Tweezers
☐ Seed beads: Blue Moon Beads
☐ Monofilament thread: Darice
☐ Hand-sewing needle

instructions

STEP ONE: After die-cutting the Decorative Accent from leather, cut a thin piece of decorative metal to fit behind die-cut openings. Apply a thin line of adhesive to the areas of the die-cut that will be covered with the metal shape; apply the metal shape and allow to dry.

STEP TWO: Fill the metal-backed openings with a thin layer of adhesive. Use a pair of tweezers to fill the openings with seed beads. Glue the bead-filled leather accent to the center of the flip-flop strap. If desired, string beads onto monofilament thread and hand-sew a beaded strand along the straps.

1

2

visual guide

Decorative Accents #6

stars

Create a stunning page like this one to showcase your own little star. Letters and stars die-cut from shiny foil and embellished with wire accents add sparkle and texture to the layout.

essentials

- ☐ Sizzix® Big Shot™ Machine (#655268)
- ☐ Sizzix Originals™ Die: #654995 Stars #2
- ☐ Sizzix Sizzlits® Dies: #654882 Sunset™ Alphabet Set

supplies

- ☐ Cardstock: Prism
- ☐ Xyron machine and adhesive
- ☐ Foil: silver metallic
- ☐ Paint: white acrylic
- ☐ Foam brush
- ☐ Pop Dots: All Night Media
- ☐ Wire: silver
- ☐ Pen: Pigma

instructions

Die-cut letters and stars from foil. To add even more interest to the stars, try scoring them, or add Pop Dots to give them extra height and dimension. You also can add paint to highlight a particular item, such as the large star shown at *right,* and then lightly sand it to reveal bits of metal underneath. Add wire accents around the stars.

visual guide

Stars #2

Sunset Alphabet Set

caught... on vacation

vacation album

Making a mini album couldn't be easier—just die-cut the pages from a variety of paper colors, cut a slightly larger piece for a sturdy backing, and embellish the inside pages with small die-cut accents.

essentials

- [ ] Sizzix® Big Shot™ Machine (#655268)
- [ ] Sizzix Bigz™ Dies: #655145 Jar; #654915 Keys
- [ ] Sizzix Sizzlits® Dies: #655170 Caterpillar; #655175 Grasshopper; #655176 Ladybugs #2; #655190 Snail #2; #655191 Spider #2

supplies

- [ ] Vellum
- [ ] Cardstock: Bazzill Basics Paper, Canson, Prism
- [ ] Chipboard
- [ ] Hole punch: Fiskars
- [ ] Xyron machine and adhesive
- [ ] Brads
- [ ] Ribbon: Offray
- [ ] Metallic silver paper
- [ ] Clear plastic
- [ ] Pop Dots: All Night Media
- [ ] Embroidery thread
- [ ] Pen: Sakura

instructions

Make album pages by die-cutting the Jar from vellum and a variety of cardstock. Die-cut one large Jar from cardstock for the page backing and one from chipboard for the album back. Punch holes through the pieces; adhere the last page to the album backing. Secure all pages with brads.

Attach the pages to the chipboard backing, sandwiching ribbon in between the layers. Cut the Jar from metallic silver paper and trim lid; use Pop Dots to secure it to the top of the book. Die-cut two keys, cut off the knobbed portions, and sandwich clear plastic between the layers to make a magnifying glass; attach with embroidery floss. Decorate the cover and inside pages.

visual guide

Jar   Keys

Caterpillar

Grasshopper

Ladybugs #2

Snail #2

Spider #2

The New

U

Independent

Emotional

Moody

Sassy

But Still Loveable

the new U

Create one-of-a-kind sparkly accents to enhance your
scrapbook pages with this creative technique using mesh tape and glitter.

essentials

- ☐ Sizzix® Big Shot™ Machine (#655268)
- ☐ Sizzix Bigz™ Dies:
  #654918 Decorative Accents;
  #654736 Sassy Serif™ Letter "U"
- ☐ Sizzix Sizzlits® Dies:
  #654882 Sunset™ Alphabet Set

supplies

- ☐ Magic Mesh
- ☐ Cardstock: Bazzill Basics Paper
- ☐ Xyron machine and adhesive
- ☐ Glitter: Sparkle N Sprinkle
- ☐ Patterned paper:
  My Mind's Eye
- ☐ Pop Dots: All Night Media
- ☐ Ribbon

instructions

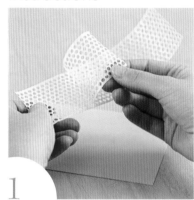

1

STEP ONE: Place Magic Mesh on cardstock with adhesive side down. Align strips to cover the entire piece of cardstock. Apply an adhesive backing to the mesh-covered cardstock using a Xyron machine.

2

STEP TWO: Die-cut Decorative Accents out of mesh-covered cardstock and then peel away the backing.

3

STEP THREE: Sprinkle glitter onto the adhesive side of the die-cut to reveal a two-tone pattern; remove the excess glitter.

visual guide

Decorative Accents

Sassy Serif Letter "U"

Sunset Alphabet Set

decorative pillow

Transform bland pillows into beautiful decorative accents with die-cut fabric shapes and beads. Cut the pieces from a variety of fabrics, then layer them for a big impact.

essentials

- ☐ Sizzix® Big Shot™ Machine (#655268)
- ☐ Sizzix Bigz™ Die: #654904 Decorative Accents #4
- ☐ Sizzix Originals™ Die: #654980 Flower Layers #2

supplies

- ☐ Pillow
- ☐ Leather
- ☐ Fabric glue
- ☐ Coordinating fabrics
- ☐ Beads
- ☐ Hand-sewing needle
- ☐ Thread

instructions

Die-cut Decorative Accent from leather and adhere it to the pillow with fabric glue. Using a variety of coordinating fabrics, die-cut the Flowers multiple times and assemble the Flower Layers. Repeat to make one large and two small Flowers. Glue the Flowers to the leather die-cut on the pillow and hand-sew a bead to the center of each flower.

visual guide

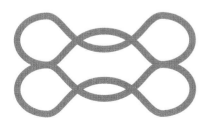

Decorative Accents #4

Flower Layers #2

charm bracelet

Express yourself with a bracelet tailor-made to suit your personality. Die-cut shapes from shrink plastic, then die-cut again to add a design to the center. Once heated with a heat gun, the pieces shrink to perfect bracelet-link size.

essentials

- [ ] Sizzix® Big Shot™ Machine (#655268)
- [ ] Sizzix Originals™ Dies: #654985 Circles #2; #654995 Stars #2

supplies

- [ ] Shrink plastic
- [ ] Pens: Sharpie
- [ ] Heat gun
- [ ] Glue pad: Tsukineko
- [ ] Clear sparkle embossing powder
- [ ] Jump rings
- [ ] Eye pins
- [ ] Beads
- [ ] Clasp-and-toggle closer

instructions

STEP ONE: Die-cut as many Circles from shrink plastic as needed for the desired bracelet length. Place the shrink plastic Circles over the Star and die-cut again. Using a permanent ink pen, write words and draw doodles around the outer edge of each Circle.

STEP TWO: Use a colored permanent pen to ink the Circle edges and then use a heat gun to shrink each Circle. Re-ink the edges with the same colored pen if needed.

STEP THREE: Press each Circle, writing-side down, into an adhesive ink pad and coat it well. Apply clear sparkle embossing powder and heat to set.

STEP FOUR: Add beads to eye pins and connect the Circles and eye pins together using jump rings. Finish by adding a clasp-and-toggle closer.

1

2

3

4

visual guide

Stars #2

Circles #2

magnet frames

Show off your favorite photos with fun, colorful frames that adhere to any metal surface. Your children will have fun assisting with this project by choosing colors and designs to reflect their personalities.

essentials

- ☐ Sizzix® Big Shot™ Machine (#655268)
- ☐ Sizzix Bigz™ Die: #654836 Frame, Jelly
- ☐ Sizzix Clear Stamps: #655032 Acrylic Stamp Mount, Medium; #654950 Backgrounds #1; #654951 Backgrounds #2

- ☐ Sizzix Sizzlits® Decorative Strip Die: #655201 Baby Says Yeah!™ Alphabet
- ☐ Sizzix Sizzlits Dies: #654763 Hearts, Paisley by Scrappy Cat; #654345 Phrase, Friends & Daisies by me & my BIG ideas; #654812 Scribbles Swirls; #654354 Star by me & my BIG ideas

supplies

- ☐ Cardstock: Bazzill Basics Paper
- ☐ Self-adhesive magnet: available at Ellison.com
- ☐ Ink: VersaMark
- ☐ Embossing powder: Stampendous
- ☐ Heat gun
- ☐ Diamond Glaze: Judikins

instructions

Cover the adhesive magnet with cardstock and die-cut the Frames. Stamp Clear Stamp Backgrounds onto the Frames and emboss. Die-cut smaller shapes, including letters, Flowers, Stars, Hearts, and Paisleys and adhere to the magnet Frames. Apply a thin coat of glaze to protect the Frames and embellishments.

visual guide

Scribbles Swirls

Phrase, Friends & Daisies

Star

Frame, Jelly

Baby Says Yeah! Alphabet

Hearts, Paisley

Backgrounds #1

Backgrounds #2

aloha banner

Use a cut-on-the-fold technique

to create letters and flowers for a fun tropical-themed banner that whips up in a flash.

essentials

- ☐ Sizzix® Big Shot™ Machine (#655268)
- ☐ Sizzix Bigz™ Dies: #655075 Flower, Hibiscus; #654716 Sassy Serif™ Alphabet
- ☐ Sizzix Originals™ Dies: #654985 Circles #2; #655169 Leaves, Tropical

supplies

- ☐ Cardstock: Bazzill Basics Paper
- ☐ Glitter glue: Ranger
- ☐ Hula skirt

instructions

By die-cutting the letters on the fold, each shape easily hangs over a purchased banner. To create the quick, custom tropical-themed banner shown *opposite*, hang each die-cut shape over the top of a purchased straw hula skirt.

Fold a 6"× 12" piece of cardstock in half. Place the fold of the paper ¼" inside the metal blade and die-cut each letter from the Sassy Serif Alphabet to spell "Aloha." Embellish the letters with die-cut circles to create polka dots and add glitter for sparkle. Cut the Hibiscus pieces, outline with glitter, and assemble. Create glittered Leaves and attach all the pieces to a hula skirt.

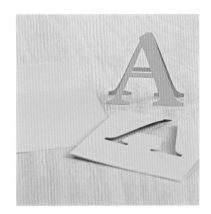

visual guide

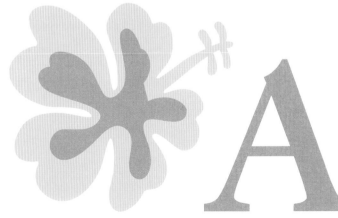

Flower, Hibiscus

Sassy Serif Alphabet

Circles #2

Leaves, Tropical

hula invitation

Get creative with a paper-pieced invitation that is as much fun to make as it is to receive. Combine colorful die-cut shapes to create the scene, then add a pull-out raffia-trimmed card with all the details.

essentials

- ☐ Sizzix® Big Shot™ Machine (#655268)
- ☐ Sizzix Originals™ Die: #655169 Leaves, Tropical
- ☐ Sizzix Sizzlits® Dies: #654760 Girl, Hula by me & my BIG ideas; #654750 Hawaiian Flowers Set; #654865 Phrase, Hang Loose w/Palm

supplies

- ☐ Cardstock: Bazzill Basics Paper
- ☐ Xyron machine and adhesive
- ☐ Hole punch
- ☐ Chalk
- ☐ Pen
- ☐ Raffia
- ☐ Sewing machine
- ☐ Ribbon

instructions

Cut a 12" × 6" piece of cardstock; fold in half for holder. With fold at bottom, punch a small hole ½" from the center top through both layers. Glue sides closed, leaving top open.

Apply adhesive to backs of colored papers; die-cut pieces for the beach scene. Shade shapes with chalk, and add pen details for eyes. Attach blue cardstock and torn tan cardstock to the holder for the water and the sand. Arrange die-cut pieces on top.

Print invitation on white cardstock and trim to 5" × 5½". Sew raffia to top and insert card into holder. Add ribbon through holes; tie into bow.

visual guide

Leaves, Tropical

Girl, Hula

Hawaiian Flowers Set

Phrase, Hang Loose w/Palm

What could be
Better than a day on the
catamaran. Cutting quickly
through the Caribbean sea
White Puffy clouds in the
Sky. Saint Thomas in the
background as we Sailed away
for a day of snorkeling,
resting, Reconnecting, and
enjoying the warm sun. The
ocean was amazing as usual
crystal clear and As we sailed
over more shallow waters we
could See all the beautiful fish
and corals. We are looking
Forward to returning
very soon.

St. Thomas

St. Thomas

Discover a whole new use for a die-cut by
transforming the leftover negative image into a clever window that reveals
the patterned paper underneath it.

essentials

- ☐ Sizzix® Big Shot™ Machine (#655268)
- ☐ Sizzix Bigz™ Dies: #654919 Decorative Accents #2; #654914 Frame, Ornate #2
- ☐ Sizzix Sizzlits® Dies: #655109 First Steps™ Alphabet Set

supplies

- ☐ Cardstock
- ☐ Patterned paper
- ☐ Rub ons: Palm tree, waves
- ☐ Ink

instructions

Cut a strip of cardstock to the desired size for a border. Die-cut the Decorative Accent onto the strip in the desired area. Cut a piece of patterned paper slightly larger than the negative image left in the strip; glue the paper behind the negative image.

Apply palm tree and waves rub ons. Embellish the strip with die-cut letters. Print journaling onto paper and die-cut the Frame, centering the journaling inside the Frame. Ink the edges of the Frame with coordinating ink.

visual guide

Decorative Accents #2

Frame, Ornate #2

First Steps Alphabet Set

tropical tote bag

Step up an ordinary bag with die-cut fabric shapes to create this chic tote. Just add fusible web to the fabric backs, cut out the shapes, and iron the pieces in place.

essentials

- ☐ Sizzix® Big Shot™ Machine (#655268)
- ☐ Sizzix Bigz™ Die: #655139 Decorative Accents #6
- ☐ Sizzix Originals™ Die: #655169 Leaves, Tropical

supplies

- ☐ Canvas bag
- ☐ Iron
- ☐ Paper-backed fusible web
- ☐ Fabric: silk, leather
- ☐ Sewing machine
- ☐ Pinking shears
- ☐ Hand-sewing needle
- ☐ Thread
- ☐ Beads
- ☐ Hot-glue gun
- ☐ Rhinestones

instructions

STEP ONE: Use a warm iron to adhere fusible web to the backs of the silk and leather.

STEP TWO: Die-cut shapes from the fusible web-backed fabrics and embellish leaves with contrasting machine stitching. Peel away paper backings and fuse pieces in place with a warm iron.

STEP THREE: Using pinking shears, cut two or three different-size circles from silk for each flower. Fold and gather pieces as shown and hand-stitch the centers together.

STEP FOUR: Hand-sew beads to the flower centers. Hot-glue flowers to bag. Glue rhinestones to die-cuts.

1

2

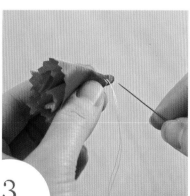
3

4

visual guide

Decorative Accents #6

Leaves, Tropical

photo ornaments

Take ordinary die-cut shapes to the next level by combining two or more of the same designs to create a three-dimensional accent.

essentials

- ☐ Sizzix® Big Shot™ Machine (#655268)
- ☐ Sizzix Bigz™ Dies: #655211 Bird w/Leaves & Flower; #654918 Decorative Accents

supplies

- ☐ Cardstock: Bazzill Basics Paper
- ☐ Xyron machine and adhesive
- ☐ Glitter: Sparkle N Sprinkle
- ☐ Ribbon: Offray
- ☐ Beads
- ☐ Eye pins
- ☐ Jump rings

instructions

Die-cut eight Decorative Accents from adhesive-backed cardstock. Cut away the bottom portion of four of the Decorative Accents and apply glitter to the tops. Attach glittered pieces to the tops of the whole Decorative Accents.

Fold each Decorative Accent in half from top to bottom. Remove adhesive backing and adhere the pieces together to make a three-dimensional shape, sandwiching a ribbon hanger in between. Attach die-cut flowers to the top of the ribbon hanger.

Hang a matted photo with hangers made from beads, eye pins, and jump rings.

visual guide

Bird w/Leaves & Flower

Decorative Accents

"shine" sweatshirt

Too often a store-bought shirt doesn't convey the message you're trying to get across, so why not make your own? Fuse die-cut fabric letters and accents onto a sweatshirt to show off your personal flair.

essentials

- ☐ Sizzix® Big Shot™ Machine (#655268)
- ☐ Sizzix Bigz™ Dies: #655211 Bird w/Leaves & Flower; #655217 Decorative Accent, Swirl; #655128 Serif Essentials™ Alphabet Set

supplies

- ☐ Adhesive-backed paper
- ☐ Paint: Plaid
- ☐ Fabric
- ☐ Paper-backed fusible web
- ☐ Sewing machine
- ☐ Iron
- ☐ Swarovski crystals
- ☐ Adhesive: Beacon Adhesives

instructions

Die-cut Flowers and Swirls from adhesive-backed paper. Using the negative images as a stencil, position the paper onto the sweatshirt. Paint the negative areas with craft paint.

Die-cut letters and Bird from fusible web-backed fabric. Machine-stitch around the bird. Remove paper backing and adhere the letters to the sweatshirt with a warm iron.

Glue small crystals to the painted and fabric embellishments as desired.

visual guide

Bird w/Leaves & Flower

Decorative Accent, Swirl   Serif Essentials Alphabet Set

dreamer

Create bold, dimensional wood-toned patterns

by die-cutting accents from paper-thin sheets of veneer and grouping

them together for a big impact.

essentials

- ☐ Sizzix® Big Shot™ Machine (#655268)
- ☐ Sizzix Bigz™ Die: #655139 Decorative Accents #6
- ☐ Sizzix Sizzlits® Decorative Strip Die: #655201 Baby Says Yeah!™ Alphabet

supplies

- ☐ Xyron machine and adhesive
- ☐ Cardstock: Die Cuts With a View, Prism
- ☐ Patterned paper: Creative Imaginations
- ☐ Scallop-edge scissors
- ☐ Wood paper: available at Ellison.com
- ☐ Pen
- ☐ Ribbon: Offray
- ☐ Jewels: me & my BIG ideas

instructions

Assemble page background with strips cut from adhesive-backed cardstock and patterned paper; cut scallop edge on one strip.

Die-cut Decorative Accents from adhesive-backed wood paper three times. Cut two Accents in half and attach two halves down the left side of the page and one in lower right corner. Attach a whole Accent next to the two halves.

Die-cut title and position it above a grid of photos; add pen details. Add bow and glue jewels to scallops.

visual guide

Decorative Accents #6

Baby Says Yeah! Alphabet

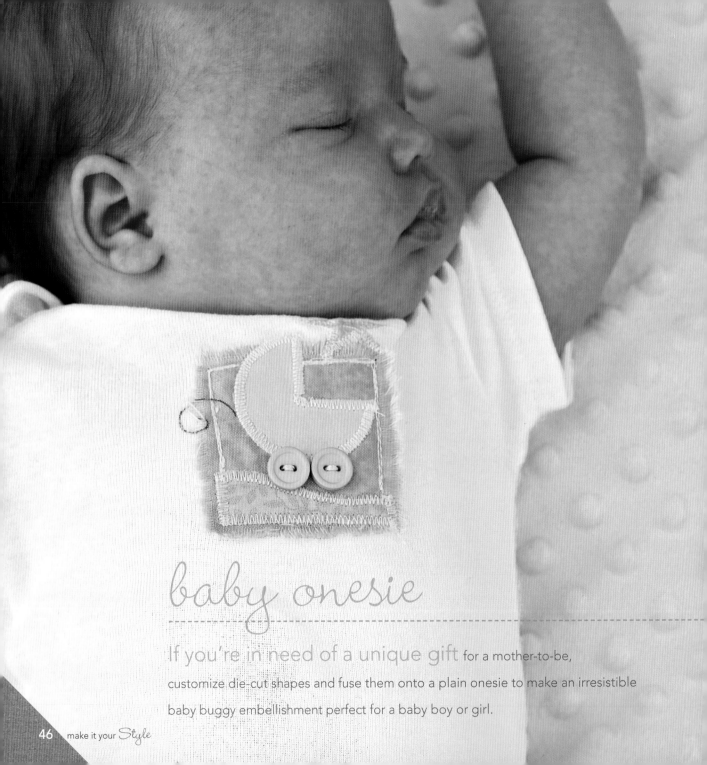

baby onesie

If you're in need of a unique gift for a mother-to-be, customize die-cut shapes and fuse them onto a plain onesie to make an irresistible baby buggy embellishment perfect for a baby boy or girl.

essentials

- ☐ Sizzix® Big Shot™ Machine (#655268)
- ☐ Sizzix Bigz™ Die: #655163 Tree, Christmas Hanging 3-D

supplies

- ☐ Baby onesie
- ☐ Cotton fabrics
- ☐ Paper-backed fusible web
- ☐ Iron
- ☐ Sewing machine
- ☐ Buttons
- ☐ Hand-sewing needle
- ☐ Thread
- ☐ Pen: Pigma

instructions

Apply paper-backed fusible web to backs of all fabrics. Die-cut semicircle from pink fabric and star from yellow fabric. Cut a small square from blue fabric and grass from green fabric. Remove a few threads from each side of the square to fray the edges.

Remove adhesive backings; layer pieces onto the onesie. Use a warm iron to adhere the pieces in place.

Using a small zigzag stitch on a sewing machine, sew around the semicircle, star, and grass. Use a straight stitch to sew a border just inside the frayed edges of the square.

Hand-sew buttons to bottom of semicircle for wheels. Draw buggy handle with pen.

visual guide

Tree, Christmas Hanging 3-D

greeting cards

Bypass store-bought cards and make your own greetings in no time at all with the help of movable dies. Small magnetic dies can be positioned inside a larger card die, making it easy to cut windows or flaps on the card front while simultaneously cutting out the card.

"hi" card

essentials

- [ ] Sizzix® Big Shot™ Machine (#655268)
- [ ] Sizzix Movers & Shapers™ Dies: #654782 Kit #3; #654945 Photo Corners, Ornate, 1 Pair
- [ ] Sizzix Sizzlits Dies: #654549 Night & Day™ Alphabet Set by me & my BIG ideas

supplies

- [ ] Cardstock
- [ ] Rhinestones
- [ ] Ribbon

instructions

Place Photo Corner dies into the Card Base die, positioning the small dies at two opposite corners; die-cut from cardstock. Glue rhinestones onto photo corners.

Add greeting to lower corner of photo. Mat photo on cardstock and slip into Photo Corners. Tie with ribbon.

visual guide

Photo Corners, Ornate

Card Base with Photo Corners positioned inside opening

Night & Day Alphabet Set

happy birthday card

essentials

- [ ] Sizzix® Big Shot™ Machine (#655268)
- [ ] Sizzix Movers & Shapers™ Dies: #654781 Kit #2
- [ ] Sizzix Bigz™ Die: #655004 Flower, Build a Flower by Scrappy Cat

supplies

- [ ] Cardstock
- [ ] Patterned paper: BasicGrey
- [ ] Rub ons
- [ ] Button
- [ ] String

instructions

Place Window Pane die inside Card Base die; die-cut from cardstock. Back with patterned paper. Add rub on lettering to the front of the Card.

Die-cut Build a Flower from cardstock and patterned paper. Layer and attach to Card front. Tie string to button; attach to Flower.

visual guide

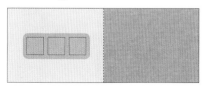

Card Base with Kit #2 (Window Panes, Three) positioned inside opening

Flower, Build a Flower

sizzlits & clearlits

CHAPTER THREE

Little in size, big on impact. You'll be amazed by the creative possibilities of Sizzix Sizzlits and Clearlits dies. Once you check out the dazzling techniques that follow, there's no stop to what you can create.

supplies

- ☐ Cardstock: Bazzill Basics Paper
- ☐ Clear beads
- ☐ Hot-glue gun and adhesive
- ☐ Floral tape
- ☐ Small paintbrush
- ☐ Paint: Twinkling H20s by LuminArte

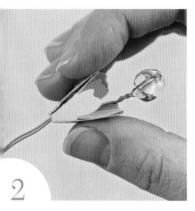

2

3

middle of the Daisy is visible.
STEP TWO: Thread a clear bead onto a length of wire; twist to secure it. Apply a drop of hot glue to base of bead and insert the wire into center of Daisy. To create the large Daisy, add two more Daisy layers to the back of each bud; secure with

hot glue. Wrap wire with floral tape.
STEP THREE: Using a small paintbrush, brush on Twinkling H20s paint on the Leaves; let dry. Hot-glue Leaves and Flowers to wreath.

visual guide

Leaf #3

Flower, Daisy

essentials

- ☐ Sizzix® Sidekick® Machine (#655397)
- ☐ Sizzix Sizzlits® Dies: #654524 Flower, Daisy; #655177 Leaf #3

floral wreath

Greet guests at your door with a pretty wreath embellished with

realistic paper blooms. Start with a purchased artificial berry wreath, then add both small and large layered flowers and hot-glue them to the wreath in a pleasing arrangement.

instructions

1

STEP ONE: Die-cut Daisies from two shades of cardstock. To build each large Daisy requires three large Daisy die-cuts. To build each small Flower bud requires one Daisy die-cut.

Create the Flower centers and buds by folding a Daisy in half and again into thirds, using the perforated lines as a guide; secure with hot glue. Open the petals so the hole in the

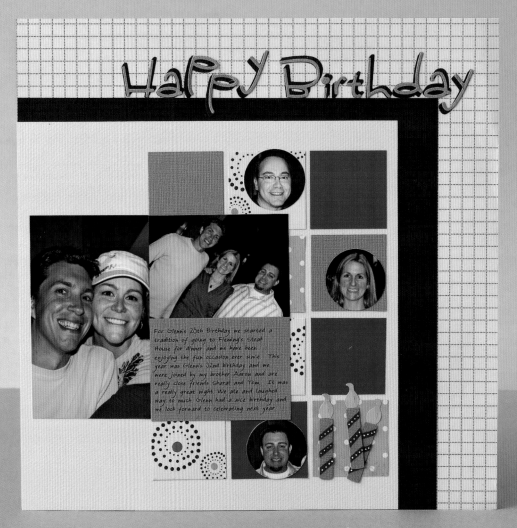

happy birthday

Make cropping photos into interesting shapes

a much easier task by using clear dies that allow you to see exactly what

will be cropped off.

essentials

- ☐ Sizzix® Sidekick® Machine (#655397)
- ☐ Sizzix Clearlits™ Die: #654407 Circle 1½"
- ☐ Sizzix Sizzlits® Dies: #654853 Candles #2; #655103 Cattycorner™ Alphabet Set

supplies

- ☐ Xyron machine and adhesive
- ☐ Cardstock: Bazzill Basics Paper
- ☐ Patterned paper: Scenic Route Paper Co.
- ☐ Pen: Sakura

instructions

Cut ten 2" squares from various patterned papers and adhere them to page background in a grid format. Using Clearlits die, cut photos and arrange on top of patterned squares. Trim and arrange two large photos and a journaling block on top of the arrangement.

Die-cut Candles from multiple colors of cardstock. Cut away detail and layer pieces. Add detail with pen and attach to page. Add a title cut from two contrasting colors of cardstock.

visual guide

Circle 1½"

Candles #2

Cattycorner Alphabet Set

floral garden topiary

Create your own blooms that will never wilt
using die-cut flowers that have been glittered, layered, and pinned to a moss-covered plastic-foam ring. Mount the ring on short twigs, then "plant" your creation in a pot for a cheery decoration that will brighten any room of your home.

essentials

- ☐ Sizzix® Big Shot™ Machine (#655268)
- ☐ Sizzix Originals™ Dies: #654980 Flower Layers #2
- ☐ Sizzix Sizzlits® Dies: #654749 Build a Flower Set; #654490 Flower Set #3; #655078 Flowers Set, Spring; #654486 Tag Set #3

supplies

- ☐ Plastic-foam ring and block
- ☐ Moss
- ☐ Cardstock: Bazzill Basics Paper
- ☐ Glitter: Sparkle N Sprinkle
- ☐ Watercolor paints
- ☐ Hole punch
- ☐ Pearl-head straight pins or corsage pins
- ☐ Thread
- ☐ Wire
- ☐ Branches
- ☐ Ribbon
- ☐ Pot

instructions

1

STEP ONE: Brush glue onto desired die-cut Flowers, then sprinkle with glitter and remove the excess. Paint plain die-cut Flowers with watercolor paints.

2

STEP TWO: For layered Flowers, place a glittered Flower center on top of two large Flowers. Crumple or curl some of the Flower Layers if desired.

3

STEP THREE: Secure Flowers to the moss-covered ring using pearl-head pins. Attach butterfly die-cuts with thread and wire.

visual guide

Flower Layers #2

Build a Flower Set

Flower Set #3

Flowers Set, Spring

Tag Set #3

Sam

Best
Friends
Forever

Sophie

best friends forever

Create a striking page border by arranging die-cuts in a puzzle-piece fashion on a contrasting background. This technique mimics the look of patterned paper while giving the layout a bit of texture.

essentials

- ☐ Sizzix® Sidekick® Machine (#655397)
- ☐ Sizzix Sizzlits® Dies: #654514 Bookplates #1; #654480 Paperclip, Flower
- ☐ Sizzix Sizzlits Decorative Strip Die: #654828 Hollywood '61™ Alphabet

supplies

- ☐ Cardstock: Bazzill Basics Paper
- ☐ Ribbon: Offray
- ☐ Jewels: me & my BIG ideas
- ☐ Pen

instructions

Make the floral-patterned side border by choosing cardstock a few shades lighter than the background paper for maximum impact. Die-cut the Flower several times from the lighter paper, then adhere the die-cuts in a tight arrangement onto the darker background strip; cut away any overhang.

Complete the layout with a sewn-on ribbon border, a die-cut title, and die-cut Bookplates embellished with jewels and pen details.

visual guide

Paperclip, Flower

Bookplates #1

Hollywood '61 Alphabet

flower hair clips

Why spend money on fancy store-bought hair accessories when you can make your own using fabric die-cuts? These little barrettes are not only great for little girls to wear, but they're a fun craft for them to make and give to friends, too.

essentials

- ☐ Sizzix® Big Shot Machine (#655268)
- ☐ Sizzix Sizzlits® Dies: #655078 Flowers Set, Spring; #654371 Spring Set #2
- ☐ Sizzix Originals™ Die: #654985 Circles #2

supplies

- ☐ Thin cotton fabric
- ☐ Fabric stiffener: Beacon
- ☐ Fabric glue
- ☐ Jewels
- ☐ Metal hair clips

instructions

Apply two coats of fabric stiffener to patterned and solid thin cotton fabric.

Die-cut Flowers from stiffened fabric. Layer and adhere the Flowers together using fabric glue. Die-cut the smallest Circle from Circles #2 using fabric or paper and attach it to the back of the layered Flowers. Die-cut another set of Circles. Fold some of the centers together for a rolled effect and add decorative jewels to the centers of others.

Glue the finished Flowers to the ends of purchased metal hair clips.

visual guide

Spring Set #2

Flowers Set, Spring

Circles #2

cake topper

Hang ten with a tropical-themed cake topper

using a miniature die-cut "Happy Birthday" banner, wooden skewers,

and cleverly placed sugars and candies for a cake that's sure to make waves.

essentials

- ☐ Sizzix® Big Shot™ Machine (#655268)
- ☐ Sizzix Originals™ Die: #655169 Leaves, Tropical
- ☐ Sizzix Sizzlits® Dies: #654755 Boy, Surfer by me & my BIG ideas; #654492 Graduation Set; #654701 Phrase, Happy Birthday! #2

supplies

- ☐ Xyron machine and adhesive
- ☐ Cardstock
- ☐ String
- ☐ Two 12"-long bamboo skewers
- ☐ Cake
- ☐ Colorful disc candies
- ☐ Brown sugar
- ☐ Blue decorative sugar

instructions

Die-cut the pennant in the Graduation Set from multiple paper colors; adhere pieces to string. Die-cut "Happy Birthday" greeting and adhere it to the pennants.

Die-cut six Leaves from green paper and poke three Leaves onto each skewer; spread out the Leaves. Roll a small square of green paper around skewer end and fray ends with scissors.

Tie one string end to each skewer; insert into the cake top. Use brown sugar for piles of sand.

Die-cut and piece Boy, Surfer from multiple colors of paper. Place on top of blue sugar waves.

visual guide

Leaves, Tropical

Boy, Surfer

Graduation Set

Phrase, Happy Birthday! #2

Many people will walk in and out of your life, but only **TRUE FRIENDS** will leave footprints in your heart.

true friends

Let your imagination take flight by die-cutting dimensional accents from transparency film, such as the butterfly wings shown here, and glittering and curling them for a pretty look.

essentials

- ☐ Sizzix® Big Shot™ Machine (#655268)
- ☐ Sizzix Bigz™ Die: #655140 Decorative Accents #7
- ☐ Sizzix Sizzlits® Dies: #654785 Build a Butterfly Set; #654374 Seasonal Set

supplies

- ☐ Patterned paper: me & my BIG ideas
- ☐ Transparency film: 3M
- ☐ Alcohol ink: Ranger
- ☐ Heat gun
- ☐ Cardstock: Bazzill Basics Paper
- ☐ Glitter: Sparkle N Sprinkle
- ☐ Pop Dots: All Night Media

instructions

Die-cut several Decorative Accents from transparency film and adhere to the top of the page background.

For the big Butterfly, apply alcohol ink to a piece of transparency film and let dry. Die-cut Butterfly parts from colored film. Slightly curl wings using a heat gun. Adhere wings to page.

From cardstock, die-cut overlay to Butterfly wings and body. Adhere wings to the body and secure on top of the transparent wings.

Die-cut three small Butterflies from clear transparency film, add glitter, and mount with Pop Dots.

visual guide

Decorative Accents #7

Build a Butterfly Set

Seasonal Set

stamped canvas shoes

Teens and kids alike will love the look of these one-of-a-kind tennis shoes. Stamped with foam die-cuts adhered to clear stamp mounts, it's easy for anyone to express their own personal style.

essentials

- ☐ Sizzix® Sidekick Machine (#655397)
- ☐ Sizzix Sizzlits® Dies: #654808 Scribbles #1; #654870 Scribbles Phrase, You Rock

supplies

- ☐ Xyron machine and adhesive
- ☐ Poly foam and acrylic stamp mount: available at Ellison.com
- ☐ Canvas shoes
- ☐ Permanent ink
- ☐ Pen: Pigma

instructions

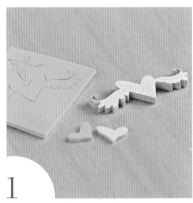

1

STEP ONE: Apply adhesive backing to a sheet of poly foam. Die-cut Scribbles #1 and the Scribbles Phrase, You Rock flower from poly foam.

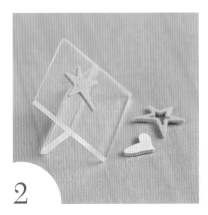

2

STEP TWO: Remove the paper backing from the poly foam and adhere the die-cut shapes to the acrylic stamp block.

3

STEP THREE: Ink stamp and apply to canvas shoe, pressing firmly but not "rocking" it. Stamp shoe all over in a random fashion, then use a Pigma pen to add doodles and details.

visual guide

Scribbles #1

Scribbles Phrase, You Rock

i love school

Think inside the box to create a 3-D accent for your next scrapbook layout. Simply use the negative space from a cutout heart image, add a clear window and backing, and fill the box with die-cut shapes.

essentials

- □ Sizzix® Big Shot™ Machine (#655268)
- □ Sizzix Bigz™ Die: #655160 Star, Nested
- □ Sizzix Clearlits™ Die: #654408 Heart
- □ Sizzix Sizzlits® Dies: #654805 Phrase, Baby Girl/Boy by me & my BIG ideas; #654551 Pep Squad™ Alphabet Set
- □ Sizzix Sizzlits Decorative Strip Die: #655112 Naturally Serif™ Alphabet

supplies

- □ Cardstock
- □ Transparency film
- □ Foam tape
- □ Patterned paper
- □ Ribbon
- □ Acrylic paint
- □ Pen

instructions

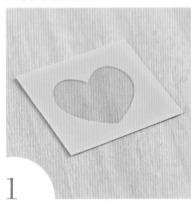

1

STEP ONE: To create the box, die-cut Heart from cardstock; trim negative into a square. Cut a small square from transparency film to fit over opening; glue to cover heart-shape space.

2

STEP TWO: Add foam tape around the back of the Heart. Die-cut small hearts in the Phrase, Baby Girl/Boy set from red cardstock and place hearts inside back of shaker box.

3

STEP THREE: Peel away adhesive backing and place the entire box on another square of paper the same size as the first. Adhere box to assembled scrapbook page.

visual guide

Heart

Phrase, Baby Girl/Boy

Pep Squad Alphabet Set

Star, Nested

Naturally Serif Alphabet

love you

Give cardstock a patterned makeover by using identical die-cuts as masks on an inked background. Remove the masks to reveal a beautiful stamped pattern underneath.

essentials

- ☐ Sizzix® Big Shot™ Machine (#655268)
- ☐ Sizzix Sizzlits® Dies: #654812 Scribbles Swirls; #655199 Tina Thinks You're Cute™ Alphabet Set
- ☐ Sizzix Bigz™ Dies: #654706 Dingbats #2; #655128 Serif Essentials™ Alphabet Set
- ☐ Sizzix Originals™ Die: #654980 Flower Layers #2

supplies

- ☐ Cardstock: Bazzill Basics Paper
- ☐ Patterned paper: Die Cuts With a View
- ☐ Repositionable adhesive
- ☐ Ink
- ☐ Felt
- ☐ Embroidery floss
- ☐ Needle
- ☐ Paper clip

instructions

Create a matchbook-style card base by cutting cardstock to size and adding a folded patterned-paper rectangle to one short edge.

Die-cut Scribbles Swirls several times; adhere to cardstock mat with repositional adhesive in a pleasing pattern. Ink entire surface and remove die-cuts to reveal pattern. Attach mat to front of card. Embellish with a cutout circle, die-cut letters, words, and brackets. Die-cut Flower from felt and use floss to stitch to paper clip.

visual guide

Scribbles Swirls

Dingbats #2

Tina Thinks You're
Cute Alphabet Set

Serif Essentials
Alphabet Set

Flower Layers #2

livin' life out loud

Mix die-cut fonts, swirls, and flowers to create a free-style title sure to capture attention. For extra interest, layer shapes and letters cut from darker hues for backgrounds and shadow effects.

essentials

- ☐ Sizzix® Big Shot™ Machine (#655268)
- ☐ Sizzix Bigz™ Dies: #655116 Boss-O!™ Alphabet Set; #655211 Bird w/Leaves & Flower; #655217 Decorative Accent, Swirl
- ☐ Sizzix Originals™ Dies: #654985 Circles #2; #654643 Frames, Rectangle Combo
- ☐ Sizzix Sizzlits® Dies: #655109 First Steps™ Alphabet Set; #654817 Retro Metro™ Alphabet Set by Scrappy Cat; #654883 Sock Hop™ Alphabet Set; #654395 Mango Tango™ Alphabet Set by Scrappy Cat
- ☐ Sizzix Sizzlits Decorative Strip Die: #655112 Naturally Serif™ Alphabet

supplies

- ☐ Xyron machine and adhesive
- ☐ Cardstock
- ☐ Brad
- ☐ Pop Dots: All Night Media

instructions

Assemble page background with strips of paper and matted photos.

Die-cut Swirls, Flowers, and letters from complementary adhesive-backed cardstocks. Place a few letters on top of die-cut Circles and Rectangles. Use a brad to attach a Flower over the "O." Mount some of the pieces with Pop Dots for extra dimension.

visual guide

Boss-O!
Alphabet Set

Frames, Rectangle Combo

First Steps
Alphabet Set

Retro Metro
Alphabet Set

Bird w/Leaves & Flower

Decorative Accent, Swirl

Circles #2

Sock Hop
Alphabet Set

Mango Tango
Alphabet Set

Naturally Serif
Alphabet

candy goodie bag

There's no need to purchase goodie bags

when you can create custom bag toppers with die-cut letters and

embellishments to reflect your party's theme.

essentials

- ☐ Sizzix® Big Shot™ Machine (#655268)
- ☐ Sizzix Bigz™ Die: #654707 Flower & Vines #1
- ☐ Sizzix Sizzlits® Dies: #654794 Cupcake #3; #654432 Phrase, So Sweet! by me & my BIG ideas

supplies

- ☐ Cardstock: Bazzill Basics Paper
- ☐ Clear bag
- ☐ Diamond Glaze: Judikins
- ☐ Glitter: Sparkle N Sprinkle
- ☐ Rhinestones
- ☐ Candy
- ☐ Hot-glue gun and adhesive
- ☐ Pop Dots: All Night Media

instructions

Cut cardstock to desired size to make a topper that fits over the bag top when folded. Cut scallops along the bottom of the topper.

Die-cut "So Sweet" from multiple colors of cardstock; cut the letters apart and select pieces for title. Apply Diamond Glaze to letters; let dry. Attach letters to topper.

Die-cut Vine and embellish with glitter; attach to topper. Die-cut Cupcake from colored cardstocks and piece shapes together; adhere to topper with Pop Dots. Add glitter and rhinestones and attach to topper. Hot-glue topper to filled bag.

visual guide

Flower & Vines #1

Cupcake #3

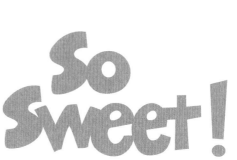

Phrase, So Sweet!

ride

Create a two-toned look using two patterned papers cut from identical dies, cutting each in half, and joining the mismatched halves together to give extra impact to a title.

essentials

- ☐ Sizzix® Big Shot™ Machine (#655268)
- ☐ Sizzix Bigz™ Die: #654738 Sassy Serif™ Alphabet
- ☐ Sizzix Sizzlits® Dies: #654817 Retro Metro™ Alphabet Set by Scrappy Cat
- ☐ Sizzix Texturz™ Texture Plates: #654779 Kit #2

supplies

- ☐ Cardstock: Bazzill Basics Paper, Die-Cuts With A View
- ☐ Digital photo program: Adobe Photoshop, Adobe Illustrator
- ☐ Font: CK Fraternity
- ☐ Ink: Tsukineko
- ☐ Pop Dots: All Night Media
- ☐ Stamps: Autumn Leaves

instructions

After embellishing background page with machine stitching and rubber stamped flourishes, arrange photos on page. Use a computer program to generate words on the smaller photos.

Die-cut large initial from white-core cardstock. Emboss circle texture onto initial and lightly sand to highlight pattern. Adhere to page with Pop Dots.

Create title as shown at *right*.

Die-cut the title out of two contrasting papers. Cut each letter in half, and adhere the top half of each letter to the main photo. Adhere the bottom half of each letter to the page just below the photo.

visual guide

Sassy Serif Alphabet

Retro Metro Alphabet Set

Texture Plate: Kit #2

photo coasters

These trendy coasters will do double duty

by showcasing your favorite photos as they protect your furniture from water marks. Decorative die-cut photo corners arranged in an interesting pattern create a graphic background pattern.

essentials

- ☐ Sizzix® Sidekick Machine (#655397)
- ☐ Sizzix Sizzlits® Die: #654804 Photo Corners #2

supplies

- ☐ Square glass coasters, either etched with grid or plain
- ☐ Xyron machine and adhesive
- ☐ Etching cream or spray paint (optional)
- ☐ Vellum (optional)
- ☐ Cardstock: Bazzill Basics Paper

instructions

If using an etched-grid glass coaster, measure the size of one of the squares and crop a photo to that size. Apply adhesive to the front of the photo and adhere it to the back of the coaster on the desired square.

If using a plain glass coaster, measure and mark a four-by-four grid on the back side. Etch or apply adhesive-backed vellum to alternating squares. Crop photo to fit one of the squares and adhere to coaster.

For both coaster types, apply adhesive to die-cut Photo Corners and decorate alternating squares with the shapes. If desired, change the direction of the dies to create a more interesting pattern.

visual guide

Photo Corners #2

for cara

embosslits,
texturz & simple
impressions

CHAPTER FOUR

Add texture to your designs and step up to fun! Sizzix Embosslits, Texturz, and Simple Impressions let you add exciting dimension to all kinds of papers—and in such easy ways. Create raised die-cuts for lettering, numbers, and shapes. Use overall designs to sculpt backgrounds and borders. Impress sweet motifs into paper. Can't wait to try them out? Take a look at all the ideas that follow and enjoy paper design from a whole new perspective.

supplies

- ☐ Gift bag
- ☐ Cardstock: Die Cuts With a View
- ☐ Sandpaper
- ☐ Patterned paper: me & my BIG Ideas
- ☐ Rhinestones
- ☐ Ribbon: Offray

visual guide

Die: Flower Layers #2

Die: Leaf #3

Die: Tag

Texture Plate: Kit #2

Texture Plate: Kit #4

helpful hints

WHAT MATERIALS CAN I USE WITH EMBOSSLITS, TEXTURZ & SIMPLE IMPRESSIONS?

EMBOSSLITS ALPHABETS AND EMBOSSLITS DECORATIVE DIES combine cutting and embossing into one easy step. Use them with:

- CARDSTOCK
- DECORATIVE METAL
- PAPER
- VELLUM

TEXTURZ TEXTURE PLATES add overall pattern and dimension to an assortment of papers. Use them with:

- CARDSTOCK
- MAT BOARD
- METALLIC FOIL
- PAPER
- PHOTO PAPER
- VELLUM

SIMPLE IMPRESSIONS EMBOSSING FOLDERS work as embossing tools and as stencils. Use them with:

- CARDSTOCK
- METALLIC FOIL
- PAPER
- VELLUM

floral gift bag

In the true spirit of giving, this happy bag is really two gifts in one. It's a unique wrap—the recipient can use it again for another gifting occasion. It's also sweet enough to serve as a centerpiece or a springtime table accent.

instructions

Dress up a ready-made gift bag by adding patterned paper, ribbon, and a dimensional Flower along the top border and replacing the handle with one fashioned from ribbon.

For the Flower and Leaves, add texture to cardstock with texture plates and then die-cut the shapes. Lightly sand raised areas to reveal the white core of each cardstock shape. Layer the die-cut Flowers and adhere small rhinestones to the center.

"friends" card

Make a lasting impression with an embossed card.

This easy beauty features embossed butterflies that are further detailed with a light sanding, shiny glaze, and sparkling rhinestones.

essentials

- ☐ Sizzix® Sidekick® Machine (#655397)
- ☐ Sizzix Embosslits™ Die: #654963 Butterfly #2 by Scrappy Cat
- ☐ Sizzix Rub Ons: #655085 Hunky Dory™ Alphabet Set #1

supplies

- ☐ Plain paper: Bazzill Basics Paper, Die Cuts With a View
- ☐ Patterned paper: My Mind's Eye
- ☐ Sticker: Vine by Sandylion
- ☐ Diamond Glaze: Judikins
- ☐ Rhinestones

instructions

Cut cardstock to size and fold in half to form card base. Cut patterned paper to size and attach to front of card base. Place sticker over patterned paper to make vines.

Die-cut three Butterflies from complementary-colored white-core cardstock and sand raised areas to reveal pattern. Highlight sanded areas with Diamond Glaze and allow to dry. Embellish Butterflies with rhinestones and place over vines.

Cut small mat from complementary colors of cardstock and attach to card base. Add Rub Ons to create title.

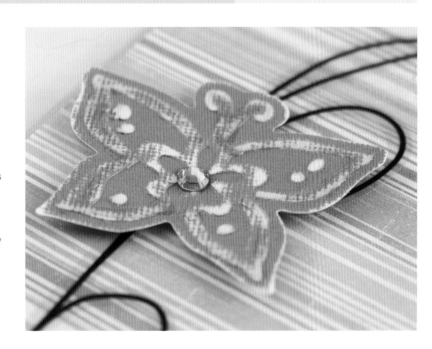

visual guide

Die: Butterfly #2

F

Rub Ons: Hunky Dory™ Alphabet Set #1

joy

You'll smile when you discover how easy it is to complete a handcrafted layout like this one using Texturz texture plates to do all the delightful embossing.

essentials

- ☐ Sizzix® Big Shot™ Machine (#655268)
- ☐ Sizzix Sizzlits® Die: #654516 Bookplates #3
- ☐ Sizzix Sizzlits Decorative Strip Die: #655112 Naturally Serif™ Alphabet
- ☐ Sizzix Texturz™ Texture Plates: #654841 Kit #3

supplies

- ☐ Cardstock: Bazzill Basics Paper, Die Cuts With a View
- ☐ Patterned paper: Cosmo Cricket
- ☐ Pop Dots: All Night Media
- ☐ Rhinestones
- ☐ Ribbon

instructions

Emboss flowers all over a piece of white-core cardstock using the texture plate. Lightly sand the raised areas to highlight the design. Cut the embossed paper into strips and adhere to page background. Add matted photo and ribbon to center of page.

Die-cut Bookplate and letters from coordinating papers and adhere to lower right corner of page. Embellish Bookplate with rhinestones.

visual guide

Die: Bookplates #3

Die: Naturally Serif Alphabet

Texture Plate: Kit #3

paris shadow box

A hand-crafted shadow box

is a great way to display your personal items,
and it's easy to create a stylish one when you
use texture plates to design your background.
Notice how the decorative metal really
reflects the light when you add texture.

essentials

- ☐ Sizzix® Big Shot™ Machine (#655268)
- ☐ Sizzix Sizzlits® Dies: #654546 Cherish™ Alphabet Set
- ☐ Sizzix Texturz™ Texture Plates: #654376 Starter Kit; #654779 Kit #2

supplies

- ☐ Cardstock: Bazzill Basics Paper
- ☐ Decorative metal: Amaco
- ☐ Metal embellishments: EK Success, Making Memories
- ☐ Pop Dots: All Night Media

instructions

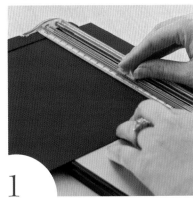

1

STEP ONE: Trim a piece of cardstock to fit the back of a shadow box.

2

STEP TWO: Emboss two colors of decorative metal and trim to create a color-blocked background pattern. Adhere to the piece of cardstock and put in shadow box.

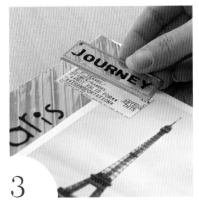

3

STEP THREE: Adhere photos and other memorabilia to the embossed background. Die-cut a title from cardstock and adhere with Pop Dots.

visual guide

Dies: Cherish Alphabet Set

Texture Plate: Starter Kit

Texture Plate: Kit #2

This year for Dad's birthday Glenn and I decided to have a relaxing picnic on the beach. We ended up heading down to Laguna and found the perfect spot to set up our blankets. We enjoyed our sandwiches and chips, but the best part was the homemade brownies. Dad opened his presents and we just laughed and took in the beautiful scenery. Glenn brought the camera and we took some great pictures. This is one of my favorite pictures of them. Mom and Dad look so happy and relaxed. We loved the picture so much Glenn got it enlarged and framed it for them. Now they have a nice memory of a great day with the family.

true love

Add texture to your pages by layering a variety of embossed images to create a unique background. Highlight the embossed areas by lightly sanding or inking them to bring out additional texture. A monochromatic color scheme allows the embossing to pop even more.

essentials

- Sizzix® Sidekick® Machine (#655397)
- Sizzix Sizzlits® Dies: #654748 Valentine's Day Set; #655200 You're My Cupcake™ Alphabet Set
- Sizzix® Simple Impressions® Embossing Folders: #654751 Flower; #654752 Frame & Flowers
- Sizzix Texturz™ Texture Plates: #654779 Kit #2

supplies

- Cardstock: Bazzill Basics Paper; Prism Papers
- Sandpaper
- Ink: Stampin Up!
- Glitter: Ranger
- Patterned paper: Scenic Route Paper Co.
- Xyron machine and adhesive

instructions

Emboss the Frame & Flowers along the edge of a cardstock strip. Lightly sand the embossed areas. Cut along one long embossed edge with scissors. Create a Flower in the same way.

Use the texture plate to emboss diamonds onto paper. Cut out a row of diamonds; brush ink over the raised image. Add glitter to the title and Flower centers.

visual guide

Die: Valentine's Day Set

Dies: You're My Cupcake Alphabet Set

Embossing Folder: Flower

Embossing Folder: Frame & Flowers

Texture Plate: Kit #2

new baby card

A baby's arrival is always a special occasion, so consider it the perfect time to create a unique card to celebrate. New moms will treasure this sweetly textured card that shows just how much you care.

essentials

- [ ] Sizzix® Sidekick® Machine (#655397)
- [ ] Sizzix Embosslits™ Die: #654964 Heart, Double
- [ ] Sizzix Sizzlits® Dies: #654807 Phrase, New Baby; #654484 Stuffed Animal Set
- [ ] Sizzix Texturz™ Texture Plate: #654377 Kit #1 by me & my BIG ideas

supplies

- [ ] Vellum
- [ ] Vellum tape
- [ ] Cardstock: Bazzill Basics Paper
- [ ] Xyron machine and adhesive
- [ ] Chalk
- [ ] A6 card
- [ ] Patterned Paper: SEI
- [ ] Decorative scissors: Fiskars
- [ ] Ribbon: Offray
- [ ] Sewing machine
- [ ] Glitter: Ranger

instructions

Emboss vellum using the Flowers from Texture Plate Kit #1. Layer embossed vellum and patterned paper over cardstock to create a background for the card front. Add ribbon across the seam where the papers meet; stitch across the ribbon.

Die-cut the New Baby Phrase from pink card stock; layer on pink-matted white card stock. Die-cut Hearts from vellum and pink card stock. Attach all elements to the card front.

Die-cut the lamb from the Stuffed Animal Set in multiple colors of cardstock. Cut apart the elements; layer the pieces. Use chalks and pens for finishing touches on the lamb.

visual guide

Die: Heart, Double

Die: Phrase, New Baby

Die: Stuffed Animal Set

Texture Plate: Kit #1

"the girls" door hanger

Design a decorative door hanger to add a creative touch to the exterior of any room. Kids—or adults—will love the message board that flips back and forth.

essentials

- ☐ Sizzix® Big Shot™ Machine (#655268)
- ☐ Sizzix Bigz™ Dies: #655128 Serif Essentials™ Alphabet Set
- ☐ Sizzix Embosslits™ Dies: #654772 Flower w/Swirl Center by Scrappy Cat; #655127 Lindsey's Diary™ Alphabet Set
- ☐ Sizzix Sizzlits Decorative Strip Die: #655201 Baby Says Yeah!™ Alphabet

supplies

- ☐ Wood strip
- ☐ White-core cardstock
- ☐ Ink
- ☐ Ribbon
- ☐ Plain paper
- ☐ Sandpaper
- ☐ Wire
- ☐ Patterned paper
- ☐ Chipboard
- ☐ Rhinestones
- ☐ Rickrack
- ☐ Button
- ☐ Cup hook

instructions

Cover a wood strip with cardstock, ink the edges, and then drill a hole in each end for a ribbon hanging loop. Die-cut letters from patterned papers and adhere to strip. Using white-core cardstock, die-cut the Flower and then sand the raised portions to further highlight the images. Attach Flowers and matted name tag to strip. Hang reversible plaque embellished with die-cut letters from cup hook on bottom of strip.

visual guide

Serif Essentials
Alphabet Set

Flower
w/Swirl Center

Lindsey's Diary
Alphabet Set

Baby Says Yeah!
Alphabet

Every fall we take the kids to Apple Country-Oak Glen. We enjoy the drive and shopping and picking apples BUT I think the most fun for everyone is having our traditional picnic at the knoll. We always have a little photo session hoping to get something for Christmas cards. My nephews love hanging with the girls and my girls love hanging with the boys.

treasure

"Whitewash" page elements to turn your design into a country treasure. A faux-effect is created by sanding the embossed flowers and the paisley-patterned paper, while the title is actually brushed with paint.

essentials

- ☐ Sizzix® Big Shot™ Machine (#655268)
- ☐ Sizzix Embosslits™ Die: #654887 Flower
- ☐ Sizzix Texturz™ Texture Plate: #654922 Kit #4
- ☐ Sizzix Sizzlits® Dies: #654817 Retro Metro™ Alphabet Set by Scrappy Cat

supplies

- ☐ Cardstock: Bazzill Basics Paper
- ☐ White-core cardstock
- ☐ Patterned paper
- ☐ Sandpaper
- ☐ Ink
- ☐ Buttons
- ☐ Xyron machine and adhesive
- ☐ Acrylic paint
- ☐ Paintbrush
- ☐ Pop Dots: All Night Media
- ☐ Ribbon
- ☐ Paper clip

instructions

To create the paisley-patterned paper, emboss white-core cardstock with the texture plate and lightly sand the raised areas. Die-cut four Flowers from white and yellow white-core cardstock; sand the raised areas. Brush ink around the tips of the petals. Adhere Flowers to the page elements using a Pop Dot, curl the petals slightly, and glue a button to each Flower center.

Die-cut a title out of card stock using the Retro Metro Alphabet Set. Dry brush paint over the letters and adhere to the page.

visual guide

Die: Flower

Texture Plate: Kit #4

Dies: Retro Metro Alphabet Set

for you

stamps &
rub ons

CHAPTER FIVE

If you think Sizzix Clear Stamps and Rub Ons are for scrapbook pages, you're right. But surprise! You're about to discover imaginative uses for both products—uses that might even lead you to entirely other crafting worlds. Check out the way Rub Ons add textural detail to die-cut letters and shapes and also how they make pretty accents on transparencies. Then see what Clear Stamps can do to a box top and a T-shirt. Now, let your imagination fly!

supplies

- ☐ Plain heavy weight paper: Canson
- ☐ Glue stamp pad: Tsukineko
- ☐ Glitter: Sparkle N Sprinkle
- ☐ Pearlescent paper: WorldWin Papers
- ☐ Small pearls
- ☐ Ribbon: Offray
- ☐ Silver rings
- ☐ Pen

visual guide

Dies: Background Shapes Set

Rub Ons: Background Shapes

Clear Stamps: Flowers

WHAT'S WHAT WITH STAMPS & RUB ONS

WHEN YOU'RE READY TO MAKE YOUR MARK, CLEAR STAMPS make the experience foolproof. Mounted onto a Clear Acrylic Stamp Mount with the help of a see-through aligning guide, Clear Stamps let you see what you're stamping and precisely where. They take all the measuring and guess work out of stamping. Use the stamps with inks or paints.

FOR EASY EMBELLISHING, ADD RUB ONS ALPHABETS AND RUB ONS SHAPES to your projects. Rub Ons easily transfer to a variety of surfaces—from cardstock and vinyl to metal, mirrors, wood, and glass. Simply cut around individual letters or motifs and then rub them in place with an applicator. Some Rub Ons motifs even complement specific Sizzlits die-cuts!

wedding favor box

Fashion one box for a special wedding treasure or make them

by the dozens to dazzle your table settings and

your wedding guests. Rub Ons, die-cut shapes, and

assembly-line crafting make breezy work of each

little gift of love.

essentials

- ☐ Sizzix® Sidekick® Machine (#655397)
- ☐ Box pattern available at Sizzix.com
- ☐ Sizzix Clear Stamps: #655033 Acrylic Stamp Mount, Small; #654954 Flowers
- ☐ Sizzix Sizzlits® Dies: #655076 Background Shapes Set
- ☐ Sizzix Rub Ons: #655079 Background Shapes

instructions

To make multiple boxes, print the patterns on multiple sheets of plain heavy weight paper, cut out the shapes, and assemble the bottoms only. For the tops, stamp images in assembly-line fashion onto all, sprinkling glitter over the stamped images while wet. Allow to dry Assemble the tops.

For tags, die-cut multiples of Background Shapes from pearlescent paper and punch a tiny hole at the top. Embellish with a Background Shapes Rub On and small pearls. Hand-write "for you" or a name in the center. Tie sheer ribbon into a bow around each box, attaching the tag with a silver ring.

wish

If you're too timid to write on your layouts or you simply think your handwriting isn't pretty, Rub Ons are a great solution for adding words—even onto the surface of a photo.

essentials

- [ ] Sizzix® Big Shot™ Machine (#655268)
- [ ] Sizzix® Originals™ Dies: #654985 Circles #2; #654995 Stars #2
- [ ] Sizzix Sizzlits® Die: #655228 Neet-Knacks

- [ ] Sizzix Sizzlits Decorative Strip Dies: #655112 Naturally Serif™ Alphabet; #654899 Small Stuff™ Alphabet
- [ ] Sizzix Rub Ons: #655080 Birthday Knockout

supplies

- [ ] Cardstock: Bazzill Basics Paper
- [ ] Patterned paper: Scenic Route Paper Co., KI Memories, Inc.
- [ ] Pen: Pigma

instructions

Adhere patterned paper bands and a photo to the background cardstock. Apply "make a wish" circles from the Birthday Knockout Rub Ons onto the photo, overlapping two circles and extending all three onto the background.

Die-cut the large Circle, the arrow, the letters for the words "Wish" and "DREAM," and two Stars from contrasting papers and adhere them to the page. Embellish with pen details.

visual guide

Die: Circles #2

Die: Stars #2

Die: Neet-Knacks

Dies: Small Stuff Alphabet

Dies: Naturally Serif™ Alphabet

Rub Ons: Birthday Knockout

"hello" card

When you see how easy it is to create your own card using die-cuts and stamps, you'll say "goodbye store-bought cards" and "hello" to designing your own.

essentials

- ☐ Sizzix® Sidekick® Machine (#655397)
- ☐ Sizzix Sizzlits® Die: #654490 Flower Set #3
- ☐ Sizzix Sizzlits Decorative Strip Dies: #654365 Phrase, Friends, Hello & Thinking of You; #654774 Swirly
- ☐ Sizzix Clear Stamps: #654953 Flower Embellishments; #654951 Backgrounds #2

supplies

- ☐ Cardstock: Bazzill Basics Paper
- ☐ Corner rounder
- ☐ Ink: VersaMark
- ☐ Embossing powder: Stampendous
- ☐ Heat gun
- ☐ Small paintbrush
- ☐ A6 card
- ☐ Decorative paint: Luminarte
- ☐ Decorative Brad: K & Co.
- ☐ Glitter: Sparkle N Sprinkle
- ☐ Ribbon: Offray

instructions

STEP ONE: Die-cut Flowers from cardstock. Stamp image onto Flowers and emboss the image with a heat gun.

STEP TWO: Using a small paintbrush, apply decorative paint to highlight the stamped images.

STEP THREE: Insert a decorative brad in the center of each Flower.

visual guide

Die: Swirly

Die: Flower Set #3

Clear Stamp: Flower Embellishments

Die: Phrase, Friends, Hello & Thinking of You

Clear Stamp: Backgrounds #2

smitten with you

Pair heart-shaped Rub Ons with precisely sized heart die-cuts, and you have a perfect combination that's charming to look at and effortless to create.

essentials

- ☐ Sizzix® Sidekick® Machine (#655397)
- ☐ Sizzix Sizzlits® Dies: #655034 Hearts Set
- ☐ Sizzix Rub Ons: #655036 Hearts

supplies

- ☐ Patterned paper
- ☐ Cardstock
- ☐ Ribbon
- ☐ Charm
- ☐ Chalk
- ☐ Pop Dots: All Night Media

instructions

Layer patterned paper for the background. Mat the photo on coordinating cardstock. Wrap ribbon around the matted photo, add a charm, and tie in a knot on the front.

Die-cut Hearts from assorted colors of cardstock. Chalk the edges. Apply Hearts Rub Ons onto the die-cut Hearts. Attach Hearts to the page, alternating the use of glue and Pop Dots to adhere them in place.

visual guide

Dies: Hearts Set

Rub Ons: Hearts

stamped t-shirt

Put some pizzazz into a plain T-shirt

by stamping flowery images

onto the front and adding your

own artistic flourishes with

contrasting paint.

essentials

- ☐ Sizzix® Clear Stamps:
  #654953 Flower Embellishments;
  #654954 Flowers
- ☐ Sizzix Acrylic Stamp Mounts:
  #655033 Small;
  #655032 Medium

supplies

- ☐ T-shirt
- ☐ Cardboard
- ☐ Paper plate
- ☐ Acrylic paint
- ☐ Paintbrush: liner or
  small round
- ☐ Rhinestones
- ☐ Fabric glue

instructions

Lay the T-shirt flat and insert a piece of cardboard to protect the back. Pour acrylic paint onto a paper plate and spread to a thin layer. Place the largest Flowers stamp onto an Acrylic Stamp Mount. Stamp into paint, being careful to not get paint on the edges of the block. Firmly stamp Flowers image onto shirt; allow paint to dry. Stamp a total of three large Flowers.

Using a paintbrush and paint, make curvy lines running from the Flowers. Use the same technique to add small Flowers and curvy lines. Attach rhinestones with fabric glue.

visual guide

Clear Stamp: Flower
Embellishments

Clear Stamps: Flowers

There are really beautiful waterfalls and perfect picture spots in the community where my mom lives. One day I decided it was time to take advantage of those areas and have a mother daughter photo shoot. Glenn was our photographer and he took a bunch of shots. We were being silly and laughed a lot. We had a great time and I ended up with some great shots of my mom and I. Every time I look at this photo I remember a really great afternoon I spent with my mom and I will treasure that forever.

moments to treasure

Special times and photos call for extraordinary accents. Here, a border of flowers is cut from transparency film and topped with matching Rub Ons and glitter.

essentials

- [ ] Sizzix® Sidekick® Machine (#655397)
- [ ] Sizzix Sizzlits® Dies:
  #655078 Flowers Set, Spring;
  #655197 Broadway Melody™ Alphabet Set
- [ ] Sizzix Rub Ons:
  #655082 Flowers, Spring

supplies

- [ ] Cardstock: Bazzill Basics Paper
- [ ] Xyron machine and adhesive
- [ ] Ribbon
- [ ] Transparency film
- [ ] Glitter paint: Ranger
- [ ] Paint: Delta
- [ ] Sandpaper

instructions

To make a border of Flowers, die-cut the Flowers from transparency film. Add matching Flowers Rub Ons over the top of the transparencies. Ink the edges and Flower centers with glitter paint. If your Flowers blend into the background more than you'd like, paint the wrong side, allow it to dry, and then lightly sand away most of the paint, as shown here.

visual guide

Dies: Broadway
Melody™ Alphabet Set

Dies: Flowers Set, Spring

Rub Ons: Flowers, Spring

San Francisco

Rub Ons easily transfer to paper and other surfaces for instant embellishment satisfaction! Here, they add texture and impact to die-cut letters and a page corner.

essentials

- [ ] Sizzix® Sidekick® Machine (#655397)
- [ ] Sizzix Rub Ons: #655086 Hunky Dory™ #2 Alphabet Set; #655097 Background, Weave
- [ ] Sizzix Sizzlits® Dies: #654526 Latches; #654554 Skooshy™ Alphabet Set
- [ ] Sizzix Sizzlits Decorative Strip Die: #654362 Hunky Dory™ Alphabet

supplies

- [ ] Cardstock: Bazzill Basics Paper, SEI
- [ ] Corner rounder: Fiskars
- [ ] Patterned paper: SEI
- [ ] Xyron machine and adhesive
- [ ] Metallic paper
- [ ] Brads: Die Cuts With a View

instructions

Add black Hunky Dory #2 Alphabet Rub Ons letters over die-cut letters of the same font. Create a large photo corner using the Weave Background Rub Ons. To create a title with a faux-embossed look, die-cut letters from the Skooshy Alphabet Set, using the same cardstock used for the background. Attach shiny die-cut Latches in place of bulky metal ones, placing brads into the holes.

visual guide

Rub Ons: Background, Weave

Rub Ons: Hunky Dory #2 Alphabet Set

Die: Latches

Dies: Skooshy Alphabet Set

Die: Hunky Dory Alphabet

embellished photo frame

Give an ordinary frame your own personal flair

with decorative Rub Ons. To keep the

focus on the photograph, choose

motifs such as these light, airy flowers.

They add individuality and sparkle to

the frame without overwhelming the

pretty image.

essentials

☐ Sizzix® Rub Ons: #655082 Flowers, Spring; #655094 Background, Girl Time by Scrappy Cat

supplies

☐ Frame
☐ Rhinestones

instructions

Cut apart the Rub Ons and apply them to the frame, creating a cluster of large and small Flowers in opposite corners for a balanced design. Add rhinestones to the centers of a few of the Flower embellishments.

visual guide

Rub Ons: Flowers, Spring

Rub Ons: Background, Girl Time

For instructions on how to make the flower shown on the cover and below, along with project ideas and information, visit sizzix.com

Ellison
25862 Commercentre Drive
Lake Forest, CA 92630-8804
877-355-4766
www.sizzix.com

Ellison Europe, Ltd.
Unit 3, Whitegate Industrial Estate
Whitegate, Wrexham LL13 8UG
United Kingdom 0870 6000625
Within UK +44 (0) 1978 264500
Outside UK +44 (0) 1978 357745 Fax
www.sizzix.co.uk